Wintertime

Wintertime is the season when the earth is at rest. From December 23 until March 20, the colder weather brings a different mood. It is a time of quiet and dormancy (inactivity). Less sunlight brings shorter days and longer nights, icy rains, or freezing winds and snow.   Some animals, like bears, woodchucks, and dormice, hibernate all winter. Many trees and other plants go into a resting stage. In winter, people change their activities, entertainment, and types of clothing.

Winter is also the season of ethnic, religious, and national holidays. If the focus is kept on the meaning of the holiday, children learn through shared rituals that they belong to an extended family who share their heritage with pride.   The recurring traditions of these holidays bring a sense of order to the child's world and offer opportunities to learn such values as generosity, tolerance, respect, goodwill, and community. Over the years, these traditions build up the child's feelings of belonging, of security, self-worth, and self-confidence.

Activities

- Invite the parents and grandparents of your students to come to class on various days and tell about their family winter holiday traditions. Encourage students to bring things that help children to remember or provide a related follow-up activity for them to take home. Have pairs of children write thank-you notes from the class to the parent-presenters.

- Make a **K-W-L** chart to determine what your students already know about winter. On three sheets of chart paper, record the following as students brainstorm:

WINTER	WINTER	WINTER
What We Already Know	*We Want to Know*	*What We Learned*
It gets cold and snows.	Why is it not cold at my grandma's house?	Winter is cold in some places and warm in others.

  The first two charts can be done at the beginning of the unit. The third can be added to daily as information is gained through books, sharing, and activities. At the end of the unit, go back to the first chart to star (*) their information that was correct.

- Discuss the concept of Jack Frost. Read *Here Comes Jack Frost* by Sharon Peters, Troll, 1981. Suggest that students look for frost at home (on windows, in the freezer, on the car). Make Jack Frost pictures and frost him with chalk or a mixture of Ivory Snow and water-based glue and glitter.

- Observe snowflakes to learn about them. Read stories and cut paper snowflakes (see clip art). Hang them from the classroom ceiling and bulletin boards.

Wintertime *(cont.)*

- Have students make chalk pictures (on blue paper) of snow families with a snowman, snow wife, snow children, snow pets, snow house. They can add a short caption under the picture telling about their snow family. Display on a bulletin board with snowflakes.

- Have students make a 3-D snowman holiday card. Students can write a greeting on the front, like Happy New Year, before gluing on the snowman. Then write a New Year's message inside.

- Make *My Winter Seasons Books* showing winter where you live. Have students draw pictures appropriate to the captions, cut out the squares, staple them together and read them to everyone in sight.

- Homework can include a record of the daily a.m./p.m. temperatures the times of sunrise and sunset, a brief description of the weather each day (sunrise 6:30 a.m., sunset 6:00 p.m., cold and windy, 210° F/99° C , snowed 3 inches).

- Show students how to make winter puzzles out of old holiday cards. Glue cards onto cardboard. Draw large puzzle pieces and cut them out. Store puzzles in fancy envelopes, and exchange with classmates to reassemble.

- Students can make a 3-D Christmas tree holiday card by cutting out four trees (pattern below) from green construction paper. Fold each in half and nest them together. Glue them along the fold. Write a greeting on the front and a message for inside. Color in bright colored balls; make glue lines for garlands of glitter.

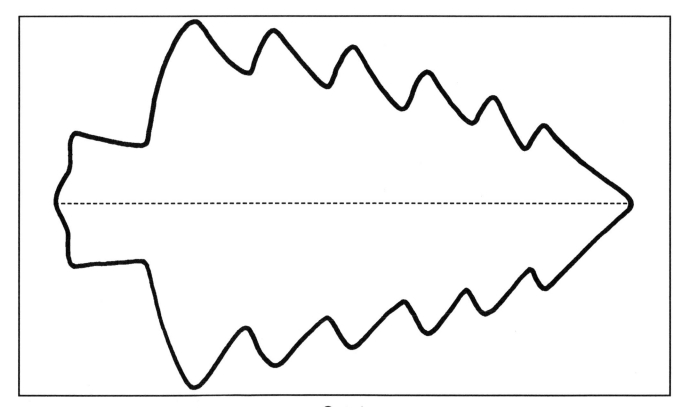

Cut 4.

A Green Christmas— A Literature Unit

Author: Theodora Kroelier

Publisher: Scholastic, 1984 (Available Can: Scholastic; UK: Scholastic Ltd; AUS: Ashton Scholastic Party Ltd.)

Summary: A family moves from snow-covered Colorado to sunny California. The children are puzzled about Christmas in California and how Santa and his reindeer will bring them their gifts. They are pleasantly surprised when they see the outcome of their California Christmas.

Related Poetry: "It's Christmas" and "Our Christmas Tree" by Jack Prelutsky; *It's Christmas* (Greenwillow, 1981); "In the Week When Christmas Comes" by Eleanor Farjeon; "Day Before Christmas" by Marchette Chute; "A Visit from St. Nicholas" by Clement Clarke Moore; *The Family Read-Aloud Christmas Treasury* (Little, Brown & Company, 1989).

Related Songs: *Wee Sing for Christmas* (Price/Stern/Sloan, 1984)

- Encourage the students to suggest the signs of winter in their general locality, i.e., snow on the ground, bare trees, cold air.

- Read *A Green Christmas* to the students with everyone listening for the signs of the two different winters.

- In small groups of no more than four, let students discuss together what winter was like in Colorado and what it was like in California.

- As a whole group, encourage small groups to report back what they discussed. Using a Venn diagram, teacher and students can chart what it would be like for both kinds of Christmases. Stress the things that are the same. Younger students may complete the activity page for *A Green Christmas*.

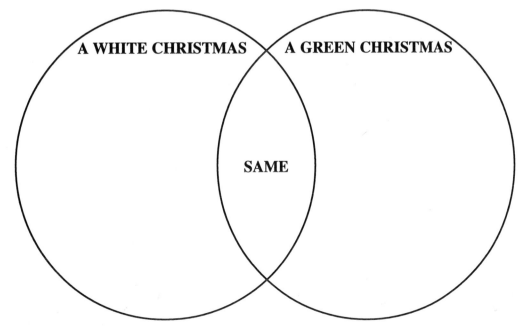

A Green Christmas
Activity Sheet

Directions: Put the words and pictures from the bottom section in the proper box at the top.

Christmas in Colorado		Christmas in California	

palm tree | woolen mittens | sandy beaches | frost on a window

walking shorts | sailboat | snow mobile | snowman

My Winter Seasons Book

My

Winter Seasons

Book

By_____

This is how winter looks where I live.

Many trees and small plants rest in the winter.

Some animals hibernate to rest in the winter.

This is how I dress in the wintertime.

I like to play outdoors in the wintertime.

This is how I celebrate in the wintertime.

The stars shine brightly at night in the wintertime.

Winter Celebrations

Hanukkah

The Festival of Lights, known as Hanukkah, is a Jewish holiday celebrated for over 2000 years around the world. Coming in late fall or early winter, Jewish families honor Judah Maccabee's victory over King Antiochus, thus winning the right for his people to worship their own God. Miraculously, a one-day supply of oil burned for the full eight-day victory celebration. The lighting of the menorah, ceremonial family feasts, playing dreidel games, giving gifts, eating latkes and applesauce, and gold-wrapped chocolate coins all have a part in this solemn family ritual.

Christmas

Christmas is a Christian celebration for which preparation starts many days before the holiday arrives on December 25: making festive plans with family and friends; decorating the home with Christmas symbols, lights, and evergreens; attending holiday choir services and parties; caroling to hospital patients, invalids, family, and neighbors; choosing and adorning the Christmas tree; carefully selecting, wrapping, and placing gifts under the tree; preparing for the Christmas feast; sharing gifts and food with the poor. Many church families attend a December 24 candlelight Christmas Eve service to observe the eve of the birth of Jesus Christ. Christmas day, December 25, is the happy celebration of the Christ child's birthday. It is a family day, giving and receiving gifts, enjoying Christmas dinner, and remembering past Christmases and loved ones.

Kwanzaa

In 1966 a new holiday called Kwanzaa was begun by an African-American professor named Maulana Ron Karenga. Kwanzaa means *first* for the African tribal celebration of the first harvest of crops each year. Observed from December 26 through January 1, Americans of African descent remember and honor their ancestors, their beliefs, and their family ties and traditions. Seven candles are lit on a kinara (candle holder), one each day for the seven guiding principles, and the family talks about the special meaning of the day. Families and friends give small homemade gifts and enjoy special foods. The last day is filled with feasting and dancing.

New Year's Eve/Day

To the greeting of "Happy New Year!" families and friends gather together on December 31 to observe the end of the old year and the beginning of the new year with hats, horns, and streamers at a New Year's Eve party. New Year's Day, January 1, finds many families making resolutions to reach a goal, watching parades, eating large traditional family dinners, and watching a full day of football games.

Winter Celebrations *(cont.)*

Martin Luther King, Jr. Day

On the third Monday of January, Martin Luther King, Jr. Day is celebrated throughout the United States to honor Dr. King, a minister, civil rights leader, and Nobel Peace Prize winner. Dr. King's real birthday was January 15, 1929. Communities have marches, parades, and speeches remembering him. Students study his life, his words, and his dream to bring about peace and equality through nonviolent means. Dr. King was assassinated on April 4, 1968.

Valentine's Day

Valentine's Day is a day to recognize the people you love. Named after Saint Valentine, a martyred bishop, it is celebrated on February 14 with the giving of red heart-shaped gifts, Valentine cards, flowers, and boxes of candies for those who are dear to you.

Presidents' Day

Presidents' Day is celebrated on the third Monday in February to honor two American heroes. George Washington was the first president of the United States, and his birthday was on February 22, 1732. Abraham Lincoln, the sixteenth President of the United States, was born on February 12, 1809. Civic groups honor these presidents with ceremonies, and school children read about them, discuss them, and make pictures and projects.

Chinese New Year

Chinese-Americans celebrate Gung Hay Fat Choy, the coming of the new year, sometimes between the middle of January and the middle of February. Their New Year's Day is also the day Chinese add a year to their age. Twelve animal symbols in the Chinese Lunar Calendar, gifts of good-luck money wrapped in red paper, good-fortune foods, Chinese lanterns, firecrackers to scare away evil spirits, and the Golden Dragon Parade are all a part of the families' celebrations.

Saint Patrick's Day

The celebration of the Irish holiday, Saint Patrick's Day, comes on March 17 in honor of the patron saint of Ireland. Sending cards, wearing green clothing, tall green hats, and green shamrocks for good luck, legends of little leprechauns who follow the rainbow to find the pot of gold, dancing a jig to Irish music, dinners of corned beef and cabbage, and town parades honoring St. Patrick make this a charming winter holiday. You don't have to be Irish to join in.

Wintertime Gifts You Make

In the winter, there are many times you can give gifts: birthdays, Christmas, Hanukkah, Kwanzaa, or Valentine's Day.   It's great fun to make the gifts and cards yourself. That way they are even more special to the recipient.

Marble Trinket Box or Vase

What you need:

For the marble mixture:

- ½ cup (125 mL) water
- ⅓ (85 mL) cup plaster of Paris
- 1 cup (250 mL) white glue
- liquid tempera paint

For simple molds:

- small box/large box
- small roll/large roll

What you do:

1. Mix the water and plaster of Paris until it is thick.

2. Pour glue into the mixture.

3. Pour a little liquid tempera into the mixture and stir lightly until it gives a streaked, marble-like appearance.

4. Pour this into the bottom of a mold first and then the sides. Allow it to harden.

To make simple molds:

1. Place the small box inside the larger box so that when you pour in the marble mixture, it will harden to make its own box form. After it is dry, remove the boxes carefully. You now have a marble trinket box!

2. On a cardboard base, place a small tissue roll inside a large tissue roll, The mixture will harden to make a cylinder. After it is dry, remove the rolls carefully, and you will have a flower vase!

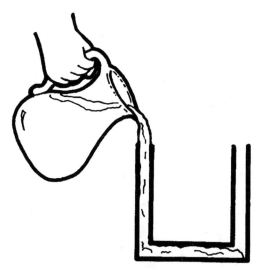

3-D Snowman Card

What you need:

- small cotton balls
- crayons
- glue
- 18" x 24" (45 cm x 61 cm) heavy construction or card-weight paper

What you do:

- Fold the paper in half.
- Color the snowman's eyes, nose, hat, scarf, and gloves.
- Cut out the snowman.
- Glue cotton balls onto the snowman's body and face but not to the colored areas.
- Write a greeting to someone you love on the front of the card and a message inside.
- Glue the snowman to the front of the card.

Wintertime Treats to Eat

Icy Snowballs

What you need:

- 1 cup (250 mL) butter
- ½ cup (125 mL) sugar
- 2 cups (500 mL) flour
- ¾ cup (180 mL) candied cherries, finely chopped
- 1 teaspoon (5 mL) vanilla
- sugar to coat snowballs

What you do:

1. Mix together the butter, flour, sugar, vanilla, and candied cherries.
2. Roll the mixture into little balls; place the balls on a greased cookie sheet.
3. Bake at 350º F (180º C) for 8-10 minutes.
4. Let the cookies cool and then roll them in sugar to make them look like snowballs.

Winter Treats

What you need:

- 3 cups (750 mL) miniature marshmallows
- 4 cups (1 L) crispy rice cereal
- 3 tablespoons (45 mL) butter
- ½ teaspoon (2.5 mL) vanilla
- candied cherries

What you do:

1. Melt the marshmallows over low heat, stirring constantly.
2. Add the vanilla and cereal; stir until the cereal is coated.
3. Put butter on your hands and shape the mixture into little snowmen or trees.
4. Press in candied fruit for decorations.
5. Let them cool. Enjoy!

A Winter Crystal Garden

A crystal garden is a kind of chemical garden that is beautiful to look at. When your crystals begin to grow, leave the garden in a place where everyone can see it. Crystal gardens make nice gifts, too.

What you need:

- 3 charcoal briquettes
- ¾ cup (180 mL) water
- ¼ cup (65 mL) laundry bluing
- ¼ cup (65 mL) salt
- 1 tablespoon (15 mL) ammonia
- 1 glass bowl
- food coloring

_____

_____

What you do:

1. Place the briquettes in a glass bowl.
2. Put food coloring on the briquettes.

3. Mix the other items together.
4. Pour them over the briquettes.

Crystals will form and in a few days, you will see a lovely crystal garden.

Draw your crystal garden below as it changes. Write the dates below your pictures.

Date_____	Date_____	Date_____

A Tiny Winter Holidays Book

What you need:

- One copy of *A Tiny Winter Holidays Book* for each student
- crayons
- scissors

What you do: (See the diagram below)

1. Cut the book along the outside edge lines. Fold the paper in half lengthwise.
2. Fold it in half again and then fold it in half again.
3. Unfold the paper (eight parts).
4. Fold it in half widthwise.
5. Cut along the center crease from the folded edge to the dot. (See the diagram below).
6. Open the paper.
7. Fold it lengthwise again.
8. Push the end sections together to fold into a tiny book. Four pages will be formed.

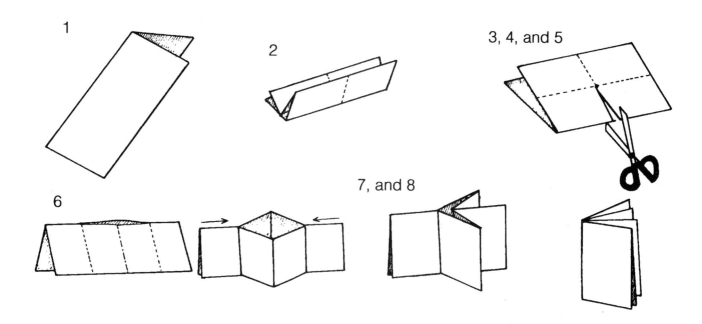

When you have finished your book, read it to your partner, your group, your younger friends, your older friends, your classroom aides, volunteers, your parents, your grandparents, your brothers and sisters, your babysitter, your dog, your goldfish, your stuffed animals and dolls . . .

Presidents' Day honors all the United States' presidents.

Valentine's Day and St. Patrick's Day are fun to share with family and friends.

By _____

Winter Holidays

Martin Luther King, Jr. Day honors a great civil rights leader.

Hanukkah means the Festival of Lights.

New Year's Day sees the next year in around the world.

HAPPY NEW YEAR

Christmas is baby Jesus' birthday.

At Kwanzaa, African Americans honor their ancestors.

Winter Clip Art

Directions: Use the clip art for making cards, gift tags, mobiles, or bulletin boards.

Winter Bibliography

Barth, Edna. *Hearts, Cupids, and Red Roses: The Story of Valentine Symbols.* Clarion Books, 1974.

Barth, Edna. *Holly, Reindeer, and Colored Lights: The Story of Christmas Symbols.* Clarion Books, 1971.

Barth, Edna. *Shamrocks, Harps, and Shillelaghs: The Story of St. Patrick's Day Symbols.* Houghton, 1982.

Behrens, June. *Gung Hay Fat Choy: Happy New Year.* Children's Press, 1982.

Burden-Patmon, Denise. *Imani's Gift at Kwanzaa.* Modern Curriculum Press, 1992.

Chocolate, Deborah M Newton. *Kwanzaa.* Children's Press, 1990.

dePaola, Tomie. *My First Chanukah.* G.P. Putnam's Sons, 1989.

Ets, Marie Hall & Aurora Labastida. *Nine Days to Christmas: A Story of Mexico.* Viking Press, 1959.

Fradin, Dennis B. *Washington's Birthday.* Enslow, 1990.

Gross, Ruth Belov. *If You Grew Up With George Washington.* Scholastic, 1982.

Hader, Berta & Elmer. *The Big Snow.* Collier Books, 1976.

Kelly, Emily. *Christmas Around the World.* Carolrhoda Books, 1986.

Low, Alice. *The Family Read-Aloud Holiday Treasury.* Little, 1991.

Lowery, Linda. *Martin Luther King Jr. Day.* Scholastic, 1987.

McGovern, Ann. *If You Grew Up With Abraham Lincoln.* Scholastic, 1992.

Modell, Frank. *One Zillion Valentines.* Greenwillow Books, 1981.

Moore, Clement C, *The Night Before Christmas.* Scholastic, 1985.

Peters, Sharon. *Here Comes Jack Frost.* Troll, 1981.

Prelutsky, Jack. *It's Christmas.* Scholastic, 1981.

Prelutsky, Jack. *It's Valentine's Day.* Greenwillow Books, 1983.

Sing, Rachel. *Chinese New Year's Dragon.* Modern Curriculum Press, 1994.

Tran, Kim-Lan. *Tet: The New Year.* Modern Curriculum Press, 1992.